MW01254212

Christmas Programs
for Children

compiled by

Pat Fittro

STANDARD
PUBLISHING
Cincinnati, Ohio

The Standard Publishing Company, Cincinnati Ohio
A division of Standex International Corporation
© 1996 by The Standard Publishing Company

ISBN 0-7847-0495-3

Contents

Hear the Joys of Christmas

Iris Gray Dowling

Come and listen on Christmas Day,
  To hear the joyful carolers sing.
Then we hear the speaker say,
  "Merry Christmas, let the joy bells
  ring!"

*(Have a carol sung by the class or
congregation.)*

Christmas Welcome

Iris Gray Dowling

Welcome to our church today.
  We're glad you stopped right here.
We'll tell the joyous message
  In our songs and poems of cheer.

God's Gift

Cora M. Owen

To a humble manger,
  Little Baby came.
Gift from God the Father,
  Jesus was His name.

Tell It Abroad

Cora M. Owen

Rejoice! Rejoice!
Tell it abroad.
Christ Jesus came,
The Son of God.

What A Night!

Cora M. Owen

What a night of glory!
  What a happy time!
What a precious story!
  Gift of God sublime.

What a precious Savior!
  What a lovely Boy!
Born on that first Christmas,
  Came to bring us joy.

Jesus Loves

Nell Ford Hann

Jesus loves ALL little children,
  It's recorded in the Book;
They would always gather 'round
  Him,
  All you got to do is look.

Jesus loves ALL little children,
  He died. . . and lives just for their
  sake;
I think His favorite time is Christmas,
  And He must love birthday cake!

Heaven Sent This Night

Marion Schoeberlein

Heaven sent this holy night,
Stars that make a silver light,
Carolers that come to sing,
Bells that in deep voices ring,
Heaven opens up each heart
So the whole world is a part
Of the Christmas mystery,
Jesus born for you and me!

Four and Fearless

Dixie Phillips

(Teacher should choose an outgo-ing confident four-year-old to recite.)

When I was three,
I used to be,
Afraid to be up here!
But not any more,
Because now I'm four,
And saying my part
Is simply "no chore"!
Merry Christmas to my mom!
Merry Christmas to my dad!
Merry Christmas to everyone,
May Jesus' birthday make you glad!

On A Peaceful Night

Cora M. Owen

It was a peaceful night
  On a Judean hill.
The shepherds watched their sheep,
  And all was very still.

Then suddenly there came
  An angel in the sky,
And spoke some awesome words,
  Of Christ to testify.

Then other angels came,
  And sang a joyful song
Of praises to the Lord,
  Which unto Him belong.

To shepherds they announced
  The birthday of the King,
Who brought salvation down,
  His peace on earth to bring.

Christmas Then and Now

Kay Hoffman

Heaven's glory filled Judean skies
  That Christmas long ago
When angels sang glad tidings
  To shepherds in fields below.

"Fear not—in Bethlehem this night,
  A Savior's born for all;
You'll find Him wrapped in swad-
    dling cloths
  And laid in a manger stall."

With trembling hearts the shep-
    herds went
  To find this wondrous thing,
And humbly knelt and worshiped
    there,
  The little Savior-king.

Wise men studying eastern skies
  Beheld the brilliant ray,
Bearing gifts they followed the star
  To where the Christ child lay.

We cannot kneel at the manger bed
  As shepherds did of old
Nor bring rare gifts as wise men
    brought,
  Myrrh, frankincense and gold.

We cannot do these things, it's true,
  "Our time" is not as then;
Still we can open our heart's door,
  Invite the Christ child in!

5

Did You Find the Savior?

Iris Gray Dowling

The wise men came to Bethlehem,
   They found the baby on the hay,
They brought some gifts of frankin-
   cense, myrrh, and gold.
   Then joyfully traveled on their
   way.

If you didn't find the Savior yet,
   There's no better time than
   Christmas Day.
You don't need to search the world
   over,
   When He's only one prayer away.

God Loves Us

Lillian Robbins

Oh, what joy is Christmas
   When friends and family come
To celebrate the birthday
   Of God's only son.

Big dinners at the table,
   And carols we all sing,
And part of Christmas season,
   Are gifts we like to bring.

We laugh and play together,
   Share love and happiness.
We try to watch our manners
   And do our very best.

They say kids get presents
   If they're good all the year.
I'm just like all the others,
   Expecting lots of cheer.

One thing is always certain,
   God loves us every one.
He gave the gift of Jesus,
   That's better than all the fun.

How I Think It Was

Margaret Primrose

I think the sky was bright with stars,
   And the shepherds sat on the
   ground
As the lambs snuggled close to
   their mothers
   And slept with hardly a sound.

Then all of a sudden in a circle of
   light
   The shepherds trembled with fear.
The sheep jumped up and began
   to bleat
   When they saw an angel appear.

"Fear not," the angel said to them.
   "It's the night of the Savior's birth,
And though He sleeps in a manger
   of hay,
   He will rule over all the earth."

The shepherds hurried to find the
   King,
   But the sheep went back to rest
While God took care of each little
   lamb
   On a night that was truly blest.

I Love the Christmas

Cora M. Owen

I love the Christmas season.
  It makes the gladness start.
The sound of carol singing,
  Puts joy into the heart.

I love the Christmas message—
  How Jesus came to earth,
To bring to us salvation,
  The reason for His birth.

I love the Christmas giving,
  Around us everywhere;
And God is our example,
  As we with others share.

God Looked Down From Heaven

Lillian Robbins

God looked down from Heaven
  At men on all the earth,
Planned many years ahead of time,
  Before Jesus' birth.

God loved all creation,
  The women, kids, and men.
He sent the world a Savior
  To rescue all from sin.

Would be a special person,
  More righteous than anyone,
But no man had lived perfect.
  It must be God's own Son.

So an angel spoke to Mary,
  "To a baby you'll give birth,
Begotten of the Spirit,
  He'll be God with you on earth."

Mary, the humble maiden
  Was not of wealth or fame,
But God sought a virgin
  To give His Son a name.

"You will call him Jesus,"
  To Mary the angel said,
And then he talked to Joseph,
  The man that Mary wed.

When the word came from Caesar
  That all the world be taxed,
Joseph went to Bethlehem.
  Mary rode a donkey's back.

And when their journey ended,
  Mary's time was coming soon.
A stable was her cover,
  Her light was from the moon.

Animals were attendants
  With Joseph at the birth
Of Jesus Christ the Savior.
  He came as man on earth.

We thank our God in Heaven,
  As we enjoy this Christmas Day.
Jesus was born in Bethlehem,
  Mary laid Him on the hay.

We love you, dear Jesus,
  Not just as a tiny babe,
But as the world's Savior
  New life to all You gave.

The Meaning of Christmas

Helen Kitchell Evans

Leader: What is the meaning of Christmas?
What does it mean to you?

Child 1: Christmas is God's love
Given to all the earth.

Leader: What is the meaning of Christmas?
What does it mean to you?

Child 2: Christmas is the time
Of our blessed Savior's birth.

Leader: What is the meaning of Christmas?
What does it mean to you?

Child 3: Christmas is a holy time,
A time to give and share.

Leader: What is the meaning of Christmas?
What does it mean to you?

Child 4: Christmas means bells ringing
And carols fill the air.

Leader: What is the meaning of Christmas?
What does it mean to you?

Child 5: Christmas means a bright star
Giving out great light;

Leader: What is the meaning of Christmas?
What does it mean to you?

Child 6: Yes, a star that led the wise men
On that special night.

Leader: What is the meaning of Christmas?
What does it mean to you?

All: Christmas means that people
Throughout all the earth
Remember in a special way
The time of His marvelous birth.

I Wonder . . .

Dixie Phillips

#1: I wonder what the cow thought when his hay he went to munch.
And found a tiny baby Boy lying in his lunch.

#2: I wonder what the donkey thought, his fur all soft and brown,
When he carried Mary to Bethlehem town.

#3: I wonder what the angels thought as they filled the sky,
I wonder if they knew He was born to die.

#4: I wonder what the sheep thought when they heard the angels
singing.
I wonder if they realized the "good news" they were bringing.

#5: I wonder what our Heavenly Father thinks of us on earth.
I know it makes Him happy when we celebrate "His" birth!

Unison: HAPPY BIRTHDAY JESUS

Christmas Action Rhyme

Iris Gray Dowling

(An action rhyme for 3- to 5-year-olds. Teach the children the actions or sign language indicated in parentheses.)

Little baby Jesus *(Cradle arms; swing side to side.)*
Born in a stable full of hay.
Let us thank Him that He came, *(Take hand from mouth as thanks in sign language.)*
Long ago on Christmas Day. *(Stretch hands apart.)*
Dearest baby Jesus *(Cradle arms again.)*
Laying in that manger full of hay.
Thank you for your love to me. *(Thanks sign; love sign—cross hands on chest.)*
We wish you a happy birthday. *(Pat chest for happy sign.)*

Jesus Came

Alyce Pickett

(exercise for 3 small children)

First Child: God sent Jesus to earth to be
A special Friend for you and me. *(points)*
Second Child: Jesus lived here God's love to show
To everyone *(spreads hands)* on earth below.
Third Child: Then Jesus went to Heaven. Now He *(looks up)*
Prepares a place for you and me.

C -H - R - I - S - T - M - A - S

Iris Gray Dowling

(Each child holds a letter and shows it when he/she tells what the letter stands for. At the end, all hold them together to spell Christmas. All say last two lines.)

C is for **Christ** Jesus,
The Baby born in Bethlehem.
H is for **Heaven's Best** —
God sent to redeem sinful men.
R is for **Rejoicing** from Heaven,
Angels sang praises to His name.
I is for **Infinite**—
God's love for a sinner, tells why He came.
S is for **Sin**,
God saw through the whole earth.
T is for **Time**,
God knew just when to send His Son in holy birth.
M is for **Mary**, the baby's mother;
She found favor in God's sight.
A is for **Angels**,
Who told good news to shepherds that night.
S is for **Savior**,
Who died on the cross in my place.
All say: What joy!
I can be redeemed by God's infinite grace.

10

Mary of Nazareth

Lillian Robbins

This reading can be presented as a poem or a short skit with the following plan.

Characters: Narrator, Mary, Joseph, Angel, Innkeeper

Props: Stool, doll

Costumes: Appropriate clothing for characters

Scene: Mary sits on small stool near side of stage.

Narrator: Mary was a young virgin maid
Who lived in Nazareth town.
She was loved by family and friends
And the people all around.
Plans were made for her to wed
Joseph from David's line. *(Angel enters.)*
They couldn't know that an angel would come
With a message before that time.

Angel: "Don't be afraid,"

Narrator: The angel spoke,

Angel: "You are God's chosen one
To bring the Savior into the world.
It's Jesus, it's God's own Son."

(Angel leaves. Mary moves to another position on stage. Joseph enters. He and Mary stand holding hands.)

Narrator: So many months had come and gone,
And Mary was Joseph's bride.
He was a devoted and caring man,
Attentively by her side.

(Joseph takes Mary by arm, goes to the other side of stage.)

Narrator: To the city of David, Joseph must go,
The donkey with Mary he led.
He stopped at an inn in Bethlehem,
A room for the night, he pled.

(Joseph knocks on door. Innkeeper appears.)

Innkeeper: "There's no place here to spend the night,"

Narrator: Abruptly the innkeeper said.

Joseph: "But Mary needs help, can't you see?
We're desperate for just a bed."

Innkeeper: "Go to the stable, it's not very far,
And spread fresh straw on the ground.
She'll be safe, except of course,
The animals are standing around."

(Mary and Joseph go behind screen. Innkeeper goes back inside.)

Narrator: Joseph never thought God's own Son
Would come in such lowly place.
But he thrilled with joy, the child was born,
He saw the Savior's face.

(Joseph and Mary enter; she is carrying baby.)

Narrator: Mary held her son in her arms,
Her heart was filled with love.
This child would grow and complete the plan,
Bring man to God above.

Christmas Critters

Dixie Phillips

(Children should wear costumes to portray the animals they represent.)

Lamb: I am the lamb so wooly and white,
I gave wool for His blanket that first Christmas night.

Cow: I am the cow all burgundy red,
I gave baby Jesus His manger bed.

Rooster: I am the rooster that crowed so loud,
When I first saw the Baby, I stood tall and proud.

Kitten: I am the kitten that purred so soft,
I watched baby Jesus from the manger loft.

Donkey: I am the donkey so stubborn and brown,
I carried Mary, His mother, to Bethlehem town.

Little One's Christmas Program

Rachel Phillips

(Mary and Joseph should be on stage for the entire skit. Child carrying a star enters and takes center stage to recite lines.)

Star: I'm the beautiful star of Bethlehem, I guided the wise men to Him.

(Four children dressed as shepherds enter.)

Shepherd #1: I'm a shepherd that heard the angels sing.
I went to Bethlehem and bowed before my king.

Shepherd #2: My father let me come on that holy night.
When I saw the angels, my heart was filled with fright,
Then the angels told us to be of good cheer,
Because a Baby had been born not too far from here.

Shepherd #3: I have watched my flock for years every night,
Never have I seen such a glorious sight.

Shepherd #4: I wonder why He was born in a barn.
I'm sure the innkeeper meant no harm.
If they would have asked me for a place to stay,
I'd make sure there was no smelly hay!

(Three children dressed as angels enter.)

Angel #1: I was so excited to sing
Praises to our newborn King!

Angel #2: As I sang my heart was full of joy,
To see that tiny baby Boy!

Angel #3: All of Heaven was beaming,
As we angels were singing!

(Three children dressed as wise men and carrying gifts enter.)

Wise Man #1: I bring to you my gift of gold,
To you my King of whom I've been told!

Wise Man #2: Myrrh is what I bring,
To you my tiny newborn King!

Wise Man #3: We have come from afar,
We followed a very bright star!

(After gifts are presented to Jesus, then Mary takes center stage.)

Mary: I want to thank each one of you,
For being so kind to our Son brand new!

Joseph: Our little one is blessed today
Because each of you came by today!

Children Sing: "Silent Night! Holy Night!"

The Manger Scene

Florence Harper Haney

A Narrator may read all the parts or children may recite the verses and be the choir for the suggested songs. You may add, delete or substitute the songs as needed.

Narrator: At Christmas time, we use many decorations to remind us of the reason for this joyous season. Some of us use colored twinkling lights and bright candles to remind us of the Light of the World, Jesus Christ. Some of us have evergreen trees, wreaths and garlands to remind us that Jesus brings us eternal life.

In some homes there is a creche, or manger scene, to remind us that Jesus came as a tiny baby. He had Mary, his mother, to love and care for Him. He had Joseph, His earthly father, to protect and teach Him. There were shepherds, who heard from angels sent by God, the wonderful news of Jesus' birth. Some scenes add the animals in the stable where Jesus was born. And, although the wise men from the East came later, some people add them to the scene with their camels and their gifts of gold, frankincense and myrrh.

Let's look at the creche *(manger scene)* we have here tonight and see how each part helps us tell the story of Jesus' birth.

See the donkey, small and brown,
Carrying Mary through Bethlehem town
Over rough streets on careful feet
To the warm stable where woolly sheep bleat.

Song: "O Little Town of Bethlehem"

Into the stable tired Mary and Joseph come,
Looking for quiet rest so far from their own home.
Here the innkeeper found a place for them
Because there was no room in his busy inn.

Song: "Thou Didst Leave Thy Throne" *(verses 1, 2, 5)*

Here is the manger filled with soft hay.
This is the cradle where Jesus will lay
After His mother Mary sings him to sleep.
Here Joseph his loving watch will keep.

14

Song: "Away in a Manger"

Mary is near, her heart filled with love,
For Jesus her baby, sent from God above.
Long promised by prophets of old,
She bore our Savior as they foretold.

Song: "What Child Is This?"

Joseph, too, is very near
Watching over the baby dear.
Joseph will care for Him night and day,
Protecting Him wherever they stay.

Song: "Silent Night! Holy Night!"

Bright angels came to the hillside that night,
Filling the air with singing and light.
They told the shepherds, "Go see Mary's boy.
He'll fill the whole world with God's holy joy."

Song: "Hark! the Herald Angels Sing"

Shepherds heard the angel's song
And ran to the manger in a joyful throng.
The baby in the stable they found
And told the glad news through all the town.

Song: "How Great Our Joy" or "Go, Tell It on the Mountain"

A special star shone very bright
To lead the wise men through long dark nights.
It led them many a weary mile
To find Mary and her little child.

Song: "The Star Carol"

Wise men, from countries far, far away,
Rode on their camels night and day.
Led by the star, each came with a gift,
Before the child glad praises to lift.

Song: "We Three Kings"

Jesus is the baby's name.
To save His people is why He came.
Born here on earth like you and like me.
Our loving friend and brother is He.

Song: "Child in the Manger"

We love You, Jesus. We're glad You came.
There's joy in our hearts when we say Your name.
Thank You for coming and showing us how
To love one another as You love us now.

Song: "O Come, Little Children" or "Some Children See Him"

(If desired, have children come forward and pick up the various figures, and allow them to ask questions or make comments.)

Prayer: We thank You, Lord Jesus, for this wonderful time of the year. As we share in the excitement, let us remember to be excited because You came to be our Savior. As we share our gifts with each other, may we remember the greatest gift of all is You; our helper, our guide, our teacher, our brother, our blessed Redeemer. As we share the joyful news of Christmas together here tonight, may we remember to share that glad news with our friends and neighbors, our sisters and brothers, our fathers and mothers. We pray You will fill our hearts with Your great love, and let it overflow to everyone we meet. In Your precious holy name we pray. Amen.

Our Hope and Promise, Too

Dolores Steger

This play may be performed as simply or ornately as desired. All action takes place in the stable where Mary and Joseph are seated watching over the baby Jesus.

Characters: Mary   Joseph
                   Star   Several Angels
                   Shepherd   Three wise men
                   Choir or Taped Music

Costumes: Night robes, bath robes, sheets, choir robes may all be used with appropriate accessories such as sashes, paper crowns, gift boxes, wire haloes, etc.

Scene 1: The Arrival of the Star
Scene 2: The Arrival of the Angels
Scene 3: The Arrival of the Shepherd
Scene 4: The Arrival of the Magi
Scene 5: Mary and Joseph Alone

Scene 1

Mary and Joseph are seated in the stable. As the choir sings "Silent Night! Holy Night!" the Star enters.

Star: I'm set in the sky as a beacon;
             The Father has placed me just so;
             I twinkle with light most amazing;
             I'm there to let all people know
             God's given the world a great promise,
             Fulfilled it this night with His Son,
             Born in a manger to Mary,
             The great Savior of everyone!
(The Star remains at the scene.)

Scene 2

As the choir sings "Hark! the Herald Angels Sing," the angels enter.

Angels *(in unison):* Hear us sing with such delight,
For it is that on this night,
Jesus Christ is born!
Listen as we trumpets play,
To announce this is the day,
Jesus Christ is born!
We've told shepherds come and see,
Come to the nativity;
Jesus Christ is born!
Now we're telling every man,
Celebrate God's holy plan;
Jesus Christ is born!
(The Angels remain at the scene.)

Scene 3

As the choir sings, "O Come, All Ye Faithful," the Shepherd enters and kneels.

Shepherd: While caring for my flock one night,
I saw a star grow very bright,
And, oh, it was a wondrous sight
To behold!

Then, out the sky, at once, appeared,
An angel, whom I truly feared;
I shivered as the angel neared,
And grew cold!

The angel said, "Don't be afraid,"
But go to where a Baby laid,
A Baby God especially made,
As was told!

I went, and there, on bended knee,
The Baby I worshiped happily,
For He had come to earth for me
To enfold!
(The Shepherd remains at the scene.)

Scene 4

As the choir sings "We Three Kings," the Magi enter; the Star, Angels and Shepherd exit.

Magi *(in unison):* For many miles we've journeyed,
Following a star,
And, now, at last, we've found You;
Sweet Baby, here we are!

Magi 1: This present, now, I give You,
This incense fragrant, mild,
But, oh, You're so much milder
And sweeter, little Child!

Magi 2: I bring You myrrh for comfort,
To soothe and to caress,
Yet, You will be the Comforter
To worlds of hopelessness!

Magi 3: Here is my great treasure,
A quantity of gold,
But You're the greatest treasure,
Majestic to behold!

Magi *(in unison):* We now must leave You, Jesus;
Our gifts we leave behind,
Except God's gift of You, Babe,
A gift for all mankind!

(Magi exit; Mary and Joseph are left alone.)

Scene 5

The choir sings "Away in a Manger." Mary and Joseph are alone in the stable.

Mary: We're all alone now with the Child;
Joseph: It was a wondrous day;
Mary: God has most surely blessed us so;
Joseph: Let's thank Him now and pray;
Both: Dear Father up in Heaven, oh,
We're grateful, God, to You,
For sending us the Prince of Peace,
Our hope and promise, too!

As choir sings "Joy to the World!" all characters reenter and join in singing.

In Bethlehem

Alyce Pickett

This simple, easy-to-produce play uses Bible texts, bells, a soloist, children's choir and a narrator to focus on the Christ child in the manger. Few props are used, and little memory work is required. Program time may be increased by singing all stanzas of the songs or shortened by omitting some of them.

Characters are children ages 8-13 except the Bible reader and, possibly, the soloist. *(The song could be recorded).* A man, using microphone, reads Scripture texts offstage. The bells ring and the choir sings offstage except for the last song.

If a bell choir is available the choir could ring the carols as the children sing; otherwise, a few ordinary bells may be rung at designated times.

Characters
   Mary
   Joseph
   Scripture reader
   Narrator *(man or woman)*
   Soloist
   Three shepherds
   Children's choir
   Bell ringers

Scene: Bethlehem stable.

Props: Manger *(cradle)* with hay. Baby doll wrapped in strips of cloth. Bench or stools for Joseph and Mary. Lantern. Shepherd's crooks *(canes).* Bells for ringers. Lectern for narrator *(Optional).* Stable furnishings are placed toward front of stage so the choir will have room to stand behind them for the last song.

Time: Christmas Eve night.

Costumes: Robes for Mary, Joseph, and shepherds.

Scriptures are from the King James Version and New International Version as indicated.

(Christmas music fades offstage as Reader begins.)

Reader*:* "And it came to pass in those days, that there went out a decree from Caesar Augustus, that all the world should be taxed. And all went to be taxed, everyone into his own city.

And Joseph also went up from Galilee, out of the city of Nazareth, into Judea, unto the city of David, which is called Bethlehem, . . . to be taxed with Mary his espoused wife, being great with child.

And so it was, that, while they were there, the days were accomplished that she should be delivered. And she brought forth her firstborn son, and wrapped him in swaddling clothes, and laid him in a manger; because there was no room for them in the inn" (Luke 2:1, 3-7, KJV).

Soloist *(offstage):* "O Little Town of Bethlehem"

(Curtain rises to show Mary and Joseph in the dimly lit stable, sitting near the manger. The Narrator stands at one side of stage. Bells are heard.)

Narrator: Ring out, Christmas bells! *(Bells louder.)*
Welcome the newborn King.
Blend your sounds with joyous praise
The heavenly angels sing.

Choir *(offstage):* "Hark! the Herald Angels Sing"

Mary *(reaches out and touches the baby, then turns to Joseph)*: O, He's so beautiful, Joseph, so special.

Joseph: Yes. *(Smiles at her.)* Yes, he is.

Reader *(offstage)*: "And there were in the same country shepherds abiding in the field, keeping watch over their flock by night. And, lo, the angel of the Lord came upon them, and the glory of the Lord shone round about them; and they were sore afraid. And the angel said unto them, Fear not: for, behold, I bring you good tidings of great joy, which shall be to all people. For unto you is born this day in the city of David a Savior, which is Christ the Lord. And this shall be a sign unto you; Ye shall find the babe wrapped in swaddling clothes, lying in a manger" (Luke 2:8-12, KJV).

Choir: "While Shepherds Watched Their Flocks"

Reader: "The shepherds said one to another, Let us now go even unto Bethlehem, and see this thing which is come to pass, which the Lord hath made known unto us" (Luke 2:15, KJV).

Choir: "Away in a Manger" *(hums first verse)*

(Shepherds enter, look at baby and at one another.)

Shepherd 1: Isaiah, the prophet, told us about this.

Reader: "Therefore the Lord himself will give you a sign: The virgin will be with child and will give birth to a son, and will call him Immanuel" (Isaiah 7:14, NIV).

Shepherd: Jehovah has blessed His people. *(Lift hands.)*

Reader: "For to us a child is born, to us a son is given, and the government will be on his shoulders. And he will be called Wonderful Counselor, Mighty God, Everlasting Father, Prince of Peace" (Isaiah 9:6, NIV).

Shepherd 3: Praise Jehovah! Our Messiah has come.

Narrator: Ring out in peals of joy *(Bells.)*
    While shepherds in the night *(Men kneel.)*
    Kneel before the manger bed
    Of Jesus, Lord of Light.

Choir: "Silent Night! Holy Night!" *(stanzas 1 and 2)*

(Shepherds arise and exit as song ends.)

Mary: Joseph, how did the hillside shepherds know about our Baby?

Joseph: I wonder. It seems strange, doesn't it?

Narrator: Ring out. *(Bells.)* Jesus has come
    To earth with us to dwell;
    Join the heavenly angel choir . . .
    Glorious glad tidings tell.

Choir: "O Come, All Ye Faithful"

Mary: The beautiful music, Joseph, what does it mean?

Joseph: I don't know, but I think it's because the Baby is very special.

Narrator: Ring out. *(Bells.)* Let all the world
    With instrument and voice
    Worship God's Son, our Savior.
    Give thanks! Praise Him! Rejoice!

(Joseph and Mary stand near cradle. Choir enters.)

Choir: "Joy to the World!"

Grandpa's Christmas Story

Lillian Robbins

Characters
Grandpa Archibald
Grandma
Sally, 3 years old
Timmy, 4 years old
Frank, 4 years old *(tall for his age)*
Mary Ann, 6 years old
Thomas, 8 years old
Marcie, 1 year old
Mother

Props: Three chairs, hearts for each child *(either candy, cookies, pillows or some other heart shaped item)*

Costumes: Regular clothes

Scene: In living room Grandpa is seated in a comfortable chair. Grandma sits close by. With Marcie in her arms, Mother goes to the door and calls.

Mother: It's Grandpa time!
(All the kids come in, dressed as if at play, remove jackets as they enter.)
Thomas: I knew it was about time for that call. You do that every Christmas, don't you, Mom?
Mary Ann: Yeah, Sally didn't even know what it was all about. She forgot we did this last Christmas.
Mother: She won't forget when she gets as old as you. She'll remember it every year and listen for my call just like you did this time.
Grandpa: Come on, gather around children. First of all, I want to tell you I love you.
Thomas: You say that every time, Grandpa.
Grandpa: It's because I want you to *hear* it and never forget it. *(Grandpa pats Thomas on head.)*
Grandpa: And I want to give you a big hug. *(He reaches out to a child.)*
Mary Ann: You do that every year, too, Grandpa.
Grandpa: It's because I want you to *feel* it and never forget that I love you.

(Each child comes to Grandpa to get a hug. Grandpa gives each child a little heart, either a piece of candy, a pillow or some other item.)

Grandpa: And I want you to *see* how much I love you, too. This heart will remind you that I will always love you, even when you grow up and get to be bigger than I am. You'll never get too old for your old grandpa to love you. And I want you to always remember this special time we have together every Christmas.

(Grandma hands Grandpa an old Bible and then sits down.)

Frank: Are we ready now, Grandpa?

Grandpa: We're ready now. *(Grandpa makes an appropriate motion toward each child as he speaks to him or her.)* You know every little child is a precious gift of God—you Sally, with your turned up nose—you Frank, with your ostrich legs—you Timmy, with your inquisitive mind—you Mary Ann, with your beautiful melodious voice—you Thomas, with your handsome face—and you, my dimpled little Marcie. Every one of you is a special gift from God.

Timmy: What about the pretend journey, Grandpa?

Grandpa: We're ready, Timmy. Now we're all going on a pretend journey, in a time long, long ago. We're going to a place way across the ocean to a strange country. There were no cars or motorcycles or trains or planes. But many people traveled riding on the backs of animals, or they walked many, many miles to places they wanted to go.

If a man was very rich, he could ride on a camel, but if he was not so rich and had just enough money to buy food and clothes for his family with only a little tiny bit to spare, he may have had a donkey.

Now we must remember that Mary and Joseph lived in Nazareth. It was a long way to Bethlehem. But Caesar Augustus was ruler of the land, and he sent out notice that everybody had to go back to where their ancestors lived to pay taxes.

The Bible doesn't tell us every detail about that journey, but considering the customs of the day, we can imagine how Mary rode on the donkey's back.

Thomas: What about camping out?

Grandpa: Well, I think it is only reasonable to assume they had to camp out, because it was such a long way from Nazareth to Bethlehem. That was the name of the city where Joseph had to go. Joseph was a good husband to Mary, and he would have taken very good care of her. He wouldn't want her to ride too long without rest. And of course he would get water for her to drink and they probably would have carried some bread or something to eat along the way.

Mary Ann: Grandpa, why did they have to travel so far? Couldn't they just mail in their tax like my dad does?

Grandpa: Well, Mary Ann, things were a lot different then. There was nobody to bring mail to the people every day the way they do now. The reason Joseph had to go to Bethlehem was because many, many, many, many years before that, a man whose name was David had lived in the city of Bethlehem. In fact it was called the City of David.

Thomas: I can just imagine Joseph going to the barn and getting the faithful old donkey. He probably put some kind of cover on his back to make a good place for Mary to sit.

Grandpa *(looks at Thomas):* You know, Thomas, before long you'll be telling this whole story for me.

Frank: Sounds like fun to me, traveling all that way and sleeping out under the stars at night.

Grandpa: Well, it may have been some fun in the beginning of the journey. Mary could sit there on the donkey and look across the fields and think about how much she loved the Lord. God had chosen her to be the mother of His Son, and now it was pretty certain that special baby would be born before many more moons rose in the sky. But I'm sure Mary thought a lot of times about how the angel had appeared to her and said, "Don't be afraid." *(Grandpa reads from the Bible.)* "But the angel said to her, 'Do not be afraid, Mary, you have found favor with God. You will be with child and give birth to a son, and you are to give him the name Jesus. He will be great and will be called the Son of the Most High.'

'How will this be,' Mary asked the angel, 'since I am a virgin?'

The angel answered, 'The Holy Spirit will come upon you, and the power of the Most High will overshadow you. So the holy one to be born will be called the Son of God'" (Luke 1: 30-31, 34-35, NIV). *(Grandpa closes the Bible.)* And when the angel finished the message from God, he went away.

Mary Ann: That was a long time before they went to Bethlehem, Grandpa.

Grandpa: Yes, it was, Mary Ann, but I'm sure she thought about that time while she was riding along the way.

Timmy: What was Joseph thinking, Grandpa?

Grandpa: Well, nobody knows for sure, but he was a good husband. Mary probably watched him and thought about how good God was to her for giving Joseph to her as a husband. Joseph would be good to the baby and they would raise him the way God wanted them to. I expect Joseph was hoping they would get to Bethlehem soon.

Frank, do you remember how tired you get on a trip, and how you always ask about a hundred times when are we going to get there?

Frank: Sure I do. I like to get out and do something, not just ride all the time.

Grandpa: Mary got very tired, too. She had been riding on that donkey a long time. She must have wondered when they would ever get to Bethlehem. Can you imagine how glad she must have been as Joseph looked ahead and said, "Mary, there it is just ahead, the City of David."

Thomas: Now they get to the inn.

Grandpa: Yes, Joseph finally sees the inn. There were many people traveling to Bethlehem at that same time, and when Joseph tried to find room for Mary to stay that night, the innkeeper said every sleeping place was already filled. So what could Mary and Joseph do?

Sally *(in a loud voice)*: Go to the stable!

Grandpa: That's right. Joseph led the donkey down to where the animals stayed. He helped Mary get off the donkey and gently led her to a shelter where she could lie down on a pile of hay. The animals didn't mind having visitors in their barn. In fact, do you know they may have been the first to know about the birth of baby Jesus?

Timmy: The sheep!

Frank: The donkeys.

Mary Ann: Maybe a dog?

Sally: And a kitty cat.

Grandpa: Well, we aren't real sure just how many animals were there. Of course we know the animals couldn't understand like we do. And they were not people of course, but they were probably there and heard the first cry when baby Jesus was born to Mary in that stable.

Mary Ann: Mary and Joseph were very happy.

Grandpa: Yes, they were filled with love for God, and love for each other, and love for this baby who was God's own Son. And God loved everybody so much He sent Jesus to be born in that stable. Mary wrapped Him in swaddling clothes to keep Him warm, and the angels said praises to God.

Grandpa *(pauses for a moment):* Now, my little children, I want you to close your eyes. *Hear* Jesus say, "I love you." *Feel* in your heart that Jesus loves you, and *see* in your minds that God sent Jesus because He loves you. That's what Christmas is all about—love. *(Pause.)* You can open your eyes now, but I want you to never forget this. God sent Jesus to live and die because He loves us. God doesn't just love little children like you. He loves big boys and girls, mothers and daddies, and grandmas and grandpas, too. He loves everybody, and that is one reason we have Christmas. Merry Christmas everybody!

(The children give Grandpa a hug.)

What Christmas Is All About!

Sarah Stuart

Cast

Billy: a young boy watching the kids from behind a bench.
Jeff: a rich, selfish boy
Scott: a boy who likes to joke
Jenny: Billy's sister who is standing beside him
Mary: funny, Jeff's sister
Carrie: a friendly, nice girl
Children's Choir

Scene: A city park on Christmas Eve day *(around 8:00 P.M.)*. A group of kids are sitting on a bench and some are standing around. A manger scene with Mary, Joseph, and gifts from the wise men.

Mary: Hey everyone, what are you getting for Christmas?
Jeff *(snobbish):* I'm getting a TV, a telephone, a CD player and a lot more.
Scott: I'm getting some clothes and my own room.
Mary: Well I'm getting a bike and some clothes. How about you Carrie?
Carrie: I'm getting a pair of roller skates!
Jeff *(proudly):* Is that it?
Carrie: No! That's the only gift I saw when I was snooping around if you must know!
Jeff: I just asked. Anyway, I know you have to be getting more. I mean what fun is Christmas without lots of gifts.
Billy *(coming out from behind the bench with Jenny close behind):* You guys really don't know what Christmas is really about do you?
Scott: Of course we do it's . . . .
Jeff: Money and gifts!
Jenny: That's not it! That's totally wrong.
Mary: What is it then?
Billy and Jenny: We'll show you. Follow us!
Carrie: Where are we going?
Billy: You'll see.
(The children walk around the sanctuary just talking among themselves for a little while, then suddenly Mary stops.)
Mary: Look at all the lights! Oh, look there's a shopping mall, and it's

open on Christmas Eve.

Jeff: Everytime I see the lights on Christmas Eve I think of all the great presents I'm getting.

Jenny: Well that's not what I think about.

Carrie: What do you think about?

Choir: "When Lights Are Lit on Christmas Eve" *(verses 1, 2, and 3)*

Scott: Well it's getting late and we gotta get home soon; so will you hurry up and show us what you want to show us!

Billy: Okay. Follow me!

(Kids walk to the front of the sanctuary and stand in front of a manger scene—take as much time as needed.)

Jeff: I sure would like to be that kid.

Mary: Why?

Jeff: Look at the gifts he got! The gold! Who gave him those gifts.

Choir: "We Three Kings" *(Verses 1 and 5)*

Jenny: Does that answer your question?

Scott: I still don't get how this is going to tell us what Christmas is all about.

Carrie: Yeah. It's just some kid in a manger.

Billy: That's not just some baby! That's Jesus Christ.

All *(except Jenny and Billy):* Who!?

Jenny: You know, the Son of God?

Mary: If that's the Son of God, how come he wasn't born in a better place?

Billy: There was no room in the inn.

Choir: "Away in a Manger"

Carrie: I think I'm beginning to understand what Christmas is all about.

Jenny: I'm glad!

Mary: This makes tonight seem all the more special you know . . . holy. Everything is just so peaceful and quiet.

Choir: "Silent Night! Holy Night!"

Jeff: I know what you mean.

Scott: Tonight does seem holy.

Choir: "O Holy Night"

Billy: I'm glad you are beginning to understand what Christmas is all about!

Jenny: Me too! You see presents don't really matter. It's remembering Jesus and doing things for others.

Carrie: Yeah. It's better to give than to receive.

Scott: I think you are right.

Mary: Well, we've got to go home before our parents start to worry.

(As they part they say "Thank you for explaining." "Merry Christmas" and other remarks.)

Jenny and Billy: Remember Christmas is about Jesus. Bye!

Choir: "We Wish You a Merry Christmas"

Wrapped in Love

Lillian Robbins

Characters
Mother Kristen
Father Kristen *(Jeff)*
Stacy Kristen—*(boy or girl)* age 6

Props: Table, three chairs, dishes and food for meal, sofa or big chair, tree, ornaments, plant, big stone

Costumes: Regular clothes

Scene I

The Kristen's family room—two weeks before Christmas. Mother is putting food on table as she sings or hums Christmas song.

Mother: Stacy, Jeff, come on in. It's time to eat.
(Stacy and Jeff come in, remove wraps, and sit at table.)
Dad: Something smells good in here. It's so cold out, I hope you cooked soup.
Stacy: But I want a hot dog.
Mother: Sorry, son. Today it's just soup.
Dad: Let's say the prayer for the food. *(They bow heads.)* Thank You, Lord for every blessing you give to us. We especially thank You for food to nourish our bodies this day. In Jesus' name we pray. Amen.
Mother: Stacy, have you had a good time this morning?
Stacy: You bet! I'm always glad when it's Saturday so I can go out with Dad.
Mother: What have you been doing?
Stacy: We went to the back of the grove and cut wood. Dad says it's going to be a hard winter this year.
Dad: And I think it's already starting. You should have seen the ice in the water holes early this morning when we went out. *(Tastes the soup.)* Yum! Yum! This is good soup.
Mother: I can hardly believe it's just two weeks 'til Christmas.
Dad: And I still don't have a job.
Mother: But you've been out every day looking for work, Jeff. You've done the best you could.

Dad: But that's not good enough. That won't put food on the table, and we're running out of time. Our little bit of savings is almost gone.

Mother: Well, we'll make out somehow.

Dad: When I got this little farm, I thought we could work hard and always have plenty. I didn't count on the hard times when the floods or dry weather would claim the crops.

Mother: But we've been through this before, Jeff. And the Lord always provided.

Dad: I know, but this is the first time I haven't been able to pick up a little day work somewhere.

Stacy: Dad, what are we going to do about Christmas?

Dad: I don't know, Son. I just hope I can get work somewhere.

Mother: I think Mrs. Sawyer wants another dress made. I'll get in touch with her tomorrow.

Stacy: Can we get a Christmas tree, Dad?

Dad: I'm not sure, Stacy. I had thought we may be able to cut one down in that wooded area down near the creek, but it looks like all the trees are way too big for a Christmas tree.

Stacy: But it won't be Christmas without a tree.

Dad: I'll check with the man down on the corner of Main Street. We usually buy our tree from him every year. Maybe if he has any trees left on Christmas Eve, he'll let us have one free this year.

Stacy: Can I help you load it on the truck, Dad?

Dad: We'll see, Son.

Mother: Our neighbor, Mrs. King, has already offered us a turkey out of her freezer, and I have those dried beans I've been saving.

Dad: At least we'll have Christmas dinner anyway.

Mother: Don't worry, Jeff. Everything will work out all right.

Stacy: Mom, what about Christmas presents?

Mom: I've been thinking about a fun thing we can do this year. Of course there is no money to buy presents, but each one of us can do something special to surprise the others.

Stacy: What can we do, Mom?

Mother: Well,—

Dad: I know. There are a lot of little pieces of wood out back that we had left over when we finished building the barn. I think we can make something for everybody with that wood.

Mother: Or you can just look around in the woods or around the house and fix up something. It won't make any difference what it is. We'll just have fun with the surprise. We'll see who can guess what their presents are.

Stacy: Mom, you are always saying put on your thinking cap, but it's going to take more than that this time. I don't think I can think of anything to do.

Dad: Yes you will, Stacy. You'll think of something. Your mother and I will help you. It will be fun. You'll see.

(Mother gets up and starts clearing the dishes.)

Mother: I better get these things cleaned up so I'll be ready to start on Mrs. Sawyer's dress tomorrow. We still have to get food for other days. We can't count on Mrs. King's turkey to keep us for very long.

Dad *(gets up):* Come on, Stacy. Let's start looking around. Maybe we can get some ideas for presents.

(Everybody exits.)

Scene II

Christmas morning in the same room. A small tree with few ornaments stands on one side. Stacy is looking around the tree, in corners of room, under chair. As he (she) hears Mother coming in, he hides behind the big chair.

Mother *(enters carrying box with decorations):* Stacy! Come on in here and help me finish decorating this tree. I have the popcorn and sweet gum balls ready. *(She starts taking things out of the box.)* Stacy, where are you? We need to get this finished. Your Dad will be here in a few minutes with the holly. *(Mom stops and looks around, then hears sobbing coming from behind the chair.)* Stacy, what's wrong? Why are you crying? *(She takes him by the hand and puts her arms around his shoulders.)* What is it, Stacy? Did you hurt yourself? Why are you crying?

Stacy *(between sobs):* I'm not ready.

Mother: Not ready for what?

Stacy: For Christmas.

Mother *(with sympathizing voice):* Oh, you don't have your presents ready do you?

Stacy *(stops crying):* That's not it. I have a good surprise for you and one for Dad, too. But I can't find a box or any paper to wrap my presents.

Mother *(sits in chair and takes Stacy in her lap):* Oh, dear. That's no problem. I thought something was really wrong.

(Stacy wipes his face.)

Mother: Let me just tell you about someone else who had no special wrapping for his gift. But it was the very best gift anybody ever gave.

Before that first Christmas day, God made plans to give everybody in the world a special gift. He was going to give a baby that would be a blessing to the whole world.

Mary would be the baby's mother. She and her husband, Joseph, lived in Nazareth. But they had to go all the way to Bethlehem to sign up for taxes. It was a long, long journey and both of them got very tired.

When they finally saw the lights of Bethlehem, they were glad. Maybe now they could find a room and get some rest. Joseph looked for a place they could sleep that night, but all the rooms at the inn were filled.

Stacy: I know. You told me about that before.

Mother: Then do you remember what Mary and Joseph did?

Stacy: They had to go to where the animals stayed.

Mother: That's right, and that very night baby Jesus was born in that stable. Now remember what I told you, Stacy, about that special gift. Jesus is God's Son, and He was born to Mary so He could be a gift to the whole world. But Mary only had swaddling clothes to wrap Him in.

Stacy: I know about swaddling clothes. You told me before. They were just strips of cloth they wrapped around little babies back in those days.

Mother: But the baby Jesus was also wrapped in love. And God shared that love with the shepherds and the wise men and with many, many people all through the years since that first Christmas.

You see, Stacy, what we give to others is not special because it is in a fine box or wrapped in beautiful paper, but when it is given with love it brings warmth and joy to our hearts.

Dad *(enters bringing holly):* Where do you want to put this greenery?

Stacy *(jumps up):* Wait! Let's have the presents first. I want to show you what I got. *(He goes out and hurries back with a green plant in a can.)* This is for you, Mom. I found it growing at the edge of the woods. It was just sorta sitting right there by itself like it was waiting for me to bring it home to you.

Mother *(gives him a hug):* It's a beautiful present, Stacy!

Stacy: And, Mom, it's wrapped in love. *(He wiggles free from Mom's embrace.)* Now wait a minute. *(Goes out the door again and returns. He hands Dad a big, bright stone.)* This is for you, Dad. It was down at the bend of the creek. I never saw a stone so big and pretty. As soon as I saw it, I knew it was just the thing for your present.

Dad *(hugs him):* What a special stone this is, too, Stacy. I can see how it sparkles.

Stacy: That's 'cause it's wrapped with barrels of love just for you, Dad.

Mother: I guess you want to see what you are getting don't you, young man *(lady)*?

Stacy: I'm in no hurry. Now I know what Christmas is all about anyway. It's not just about presents and turkey. It's all about love.

32

The Greatest Gift of All!

Judy Carlsen

This play is designed for a small church so that every child, Beginner through sixth grade, can participate. No special lighting is needed, but a spotlight may be used. Each class goes up on stage in turn and then remains on stage, sitting on stairs or risers.

Props: A decorated Christmas tree is an important prop for the play. Most churches will have one on or near the platform during the Christmas season anyway, so it will become a natural part of the play. Also central to the play is a nativity scene—the larger the better, so that the audience can see the figures. If a large, unbreakable nativity set is not available, good-sized cardboard figures can be substitutes. Five brightly-decorated boxes will also be needed in which the five "gifts" are placed. These "gifts" will already be placed under the Christmas tree as the program begins.

Introduction

Narrator #1: What is the best gift you ever received? Everyone enjoys receiving gifts—especially at Christmas time.

Narrator #2: Gifts are given because we love and care about someone. We spend time and money to find just the right thing to give each person on our gift list.

Narrator #1: Then, we wrap the gift in colorful paper and sneak it under the Christmas tree.

Narrator #2: Tonight we would like to tell you about the special gifts that are under our church's Christmas tree.

Narrator #1: One of them is the greatest gift of all!

Scene 1

(Fifth and sixth graders come up on stage, #1 stopping to pick up their gift from under the tree.)

#I: I wonder what could be in our package? *(He sets the package down on the stage and opens the top, brings out an angel.)*

#2: An angel! *(He places the angel either on top of the stable or in front for all to see.)*

#3: What does an angel have to do with Christmas?

James **#4:** You know—"Hark! the Herald Angels Sing." They told of Jesus' birth.

E **#3:** That's true.

J. **#5:** Even before Jesus was born, though, there were angels involved. Remember when the angel came to Mary and told her she would have the baby Jesus?

C **#6:** Right! And the same angel told Joseph to go ahead and marry her, because the baby was from God.

E. **#3:** Hey, that's right! Angels are God's messengers, so I guess they were doing their job.

C **#4:** I wonder what's in the other presents under the tree?

(They walk up onto the risers and sit down.)

Scene 2

(Third and fourth graders come up on stage. #1 picks up their package from under the tree.)

J. **#1:** Wow, this present is heavy! *(He lays it down on the stage and opens up the top, bringing out the three wise men.)* No wonder—three guys!

N. **#2:** We three kings.

E. **#3:** Of course, we don't know how many there really were. We don't know that they were kings either.

James **#4:** Well, what *do* we know about them?

N. **#2:** They were wise men who studied the stars.

J. **#1:** We know they were from the East somewhere.

James **#4:** They followed the special star from the East to Bethlehem, right?

E **#3:** That's true. But, the night Jesus was born, the wise men had not arrived yet.

N. **#2:** They visited Jesus when He was a young boy, the Bible says.

C. **#5:** Then let's place the wise men far away over here.

(He places the wise men as far away from the stable as possible.)

J. **#1:** They brought Jesus some great gifts, didn't they? Gold . . .

N. **#2:** Frankincense . . .

E. **#3:** And myrrh.

c. **#5:** These men lived far away from Bethlehem. Maybe God wanted to show that Jesus came to save the whole world.

(They walk up onto risers and sit in front of fifth and sixth graders. All the children on the stage stand together to sing.)

Song: "He Is the Way"

Scene 3

(Second graders come up on stage, #1 picking up gift from under the tree.)
#1: First we had angels, then the wise men. I wonder what our ~~this~~ gift is?
    (He lays gift on stage and opens up top, pulling out Mary and Joseph.)
#2: It's Mary and Joseph!
#3: They are an important part of God's gift to us at Christmas.
#4: Mary was Jesus' mother.
#5: And Joseph married her and became Jesus' earthly father.
#6: Jesus needed a mother and father while He was here on earth to
    teach Him how to work as a carpenter . . .
#1: To teach Jesus the Law . . .
#2: And to give Him hugs!
#3: They were the first ones to give Jesus their love.
#4: I wonder how they felt the night Jesus was born?
#5: I think they were excited—and a little scared.
#6: It's hard to be a mother or dad, even for God's perfect Son!
(They sit down on risers too.)

Scene 4

(First graders come up, #1 picking up gift from under tree.)
#1: I wonder who is in our ~~this~~ package? *(He opens it up and brings out the
    shepherds.)*
#2: It's the shepherds! *(He places them near the stable.)*
(All spread out across the stage.)
#1: God sent His angels on that night
    To tell the greatest news—
#2: "Jesus is born in a stable bed
    And brings peace to all of you."
#3: The shepherds went and bowed before
    That Baby, God's own Son.
#4: Then joyfully went and told the news:
    "God loves each and every one!"
(Second graders stand and join first graders on stage to sing.)
Song: "Go Tell It on the Mountain"
(They sit down on risers.)

*(If spotlight is being used, turn down other stage lights and have spotlight
on the following special number.)*
Song: "What Child Is This?" or "The Birthday of a King"

(This is especially effective as an instrumental solo or duet or a solo sung by an older child, teen or adult.)

Scene 5

(Kindergarteners and Beginners come up on stage. #1 picks up package from under tree.)
#1 *(he opens package):* It's baby Jesus!
(#2 places baby Jesus in the manger. All the younger children stand across the stage.)
All: Jesus is God's greatest gift of all!
#1: Little baby Jesus in the manger, I love You.
#2: You came to earth to save us. I love You.
#3: Wise men saw the star and followed. I love You.
#4: Angels told the shepherds. I love You.
(First graders stand up again and join the younger ones to sing.)
Song: "Away in a Manger" *(with motions)*
(After singing, they sit down on risers.)

Closing

Narrator #1: The greatest Gift of all is God's Son, Jesus. He came to earth because He loves you and me.

Narrator #2: Jesus died on the cross for your sins and for mine, because of that love.

Narrator #1: Only He could be the perfect sacrifice. You and I deserved to die for our own sins.

Narrator #2: But Jesus took our place on the cross.
(All children stand to sing together.)
Song: "Mary's Boy Child"
Song: "O Come, Let Us Adore Him" *(verses 1 and 4—"For He alone is worthy")*
Song: "He Is Lord"

Narrator #1: Now is the time to thank God for Jesus, the greatest gift of all.

Narrator #2: Now is the time to believe and obey Jesus as your Savior— the greatest gift of all.

Keeping Christ in Christmas

Deanne Bloesser

This Christmas program can be designed to include any number of characters by splitting the child and teenager parts as needed.

Characters

Speaker	Carol Leader
Mother	Mary
Father	Joseph
Grandmother	Angels
Grandfather	Shepherds
Child *(can be as many parts as needed)*	
Teenager *(can be as many parts as needed)*	

The first scene is the living room of the family's home. The second scene is a nativity scene at church.

Scriptures are from the King James Version.

Scene opens with Grandfather sitting at a table reading his Bible. Grandmother is sitting in her rocking chair with her sewing. Children are playing games. Mother and Father are watching with enjoyment.

Speaker: Many of the things we do to celebrate Christmas are customs from many countries from long ago. Some of these customs began even before the birth of Christ. Some originally were from pagan beliefs that Christians accepted because of stubbornness to let go of "tradition". But today as Christians, each thing we do should remind us of Christ.

Child: Let's finish decorating the Christmas tree.

Child: Let's light the candles.

Mother: That's a wonderful idea. We should have just enough time to finish before we leave for the service at church.

(Mother, Father and some children gather around tree and work on lights. The other children light candles that have been placed in windows around the church and on stage.)

Father: I read that Martin Luther was the first person to have a Christmas tree in his home. The story said that as he was on his way home one Christmas Eve, he watched the starlight gleaming on the

37

snow-covered pines. When he reached home, he tried to describe the sight to his family. Finally, he decided he'd just have to show them. So he cut down a fir tree, brought it into the house, tied candles to the branches and lit them to show his children how the trees had glistened in the starlight.

Mother: The starlight that night could have been like the starry skies of Bethlehem that holy night when Christ was born.

Child: It was one of those stars that led the wise men to the Christ child.

Teenager: The candles can also remind us that Christ is the Light of the World. The birth of Christ brought enlightenment to the world.

Child: We put lights on cake when it is somebody's birthday. The lights on the Christmas tree tell us that it is Jesus' birthday.

Child: Light helps us to find our way. Jesus helps us see how much God loves us.

Grandfather: When I see the lights of Christmas, I'm reminded of Matthew 5:14-16 that says we are the light of the world and that we should let our light so shine before men that they may see our good works and glorify our Father which is in Heaven.

Father: I think we're ready to let our Christmas lights shine.

Child: I'll turn off the lights. *(Goes to turn off lights.)*

(As house lights go off, tree lights come on.)

Everyone: Ooooo! Aaaah! How pretty! . . . .

(Family continues to put decorations on the tree.)

Teenager: The tree could be a reminder of sin, for it was through a tree in the Garden of Eden that sin came into the world. Adam and Eve disobeyed God and ate the fruit of that tree.

Mother: The red ornaments remind me that our sins are as scarlet.

Grandmother: The red ribbon and garland reminds us that we are in the bondage of sin.

Father: But it was also through a tree—the tree that was made into the cross on which Jesus died—that salvation came to us.

Mother: Then the white ornaments can remind us of the holy, clean and perfect life Jesus lived.

Child: Look. Our fir tree has branches with tips in the shape of a cross.

Child: The green reminds me of everlasting life because green is the color of living things.

Grandmother: Holly also symbolizes the promise of eternal life. It keeps its green leaves throughout the year.

Child: Its leaves are prickly like the crown of thorns Jesus wore.

Child: And the berries are red like Jesus' blood.

Grandfather: Psalms 92:12-15 says, "The righteous shall flourish like the palm tree: he shall grow like a cedar in Lebanon. Those that be planted in the house of the Lord shall flourish in the courts of our God.

They shall still bring forth fruit in old age; they shall be fat and flourishing; to show that the Lord is upright."

(Father lifts child to put star on top of tree.)

Teenager: The star at the top of the tree reminds us of the great power and majesty of God.

Mother: Stars make us look beyond our small world toward the infinity of Heaven.

Child: Christ is the bright and morning star.

Child: The five points of the star remind me of Christ—a head, two legs and two outstretched arms. *(Child stretches out arms).*

Father: It looks like the tree is all done.

Child: It seems much prettier than ever before.

Mother: Perhaps that is because now when we see it, we see more than just a Christmas tree.

Child: Let's put out the gifts.

(Children leave and come back carrying gifts that they place under the tree.)

Child: Gifts were given to the Christ child by the wise men. Their gifts were gold, frankincense and myrrh.

Father: Gold was symbolic of His kingdom. Frankincense symbolized His life on earth; and myrrh was the symbol of His crucifixion.

Grandmother: Christmas moves us to think of others and have consideration for them. Through gifts we can express our love for our family and friends. I especially enjoy Christmas cards. Their friendly messages bring cheer. They express "good will to men".

Teenager: Gifts are a reminder of the birth of Christ—God's gift to mankind.

Child: I'm hungry.

Child: Can we have some candy now?

Mother: Of course. *(Passes out candy to everyone.)*

(First child takes a candy cane and says:)

Child: How can my candy cane remind me of Jesus?

Grandfather: Well, the stick is white, hard candy. White reminds us of the virgin birth and the sinless nature of Jesus; and the hardness reminds us of the solid rock, the foundation of the church, and the firmness of the promises of God.

Teenager: The form of a "J" can represent the precious name of Jesus, who came to earth as our Savior.

Father: It could also represent the staff of the Good Shepherd. He uses it to reach down into the ditches of the world to lift out the fallen lambs who, like all sheep, have gone astray.

Grandmother: The three small stripes remind me of the stripes of the scourging Jesus received.

Mother: And the large red stripe can be for the blood shed by Christ on the cross so that we could have the promise of eternal life.

Child: And it is so "sweet" to trust in Jesus.

Grandfather: Listen.

(The carol leader is standing in front of the church congregation who are watching the program. The congregation serves as carolers.)

Carol Leader: All right carolers. This is our last stop. Let's sing "Hark! the Herald Angels Sing."

(As congregation sings, family stands together at doorway to listen. As the song ends, the family waves and shouts "Thank you" and "See you at church, later". As the family moves back into the living room, the church bell begins to ring.)

Child: Do you hear the church bell?

Father: Bells are a joyful part of Christmas, too. They call believers to worship and announce the joy of Christ's birth.

Child: The Christmas songs we sing and the bells that ring make me happy.

Grandfather: Yes. Psalm 100:1, 2 states, "Make a joyful noise unto the Lord, all ye lands. Serve the Lord with gladness: come before his presence with singing."

Grandmother: And Psalm 69:30 says, "I will praise the name of God with a song."

Child: I love to sing songs of praises to the Christ child.

(Grandmother rises from chair.)

Grandmother: Let's hurry. We don't want to be late for the special Christmas service at church.

(All exit the stage. They reenter the church from the front door, they greet people and then are seated. While the family is "on their way to church", props from the living room scene are replaced with props for the manger scene. Choir enters. The special Christmas service at church begins.)

Speaker: Welcome everyone to our Christmas service. We pray that this Christmas will be a special reminder of God's love for you. As we celebrate the Christmas season, let us keep our thoughts on Christ—the true reason for our celebration.

Choir: "Oh, Magnify the Lord"

(Choir goes down. Pageant begins.)

Speaker: *(Reads Luke 2:1-7.)*

(Mary, Joseph, baby, angels and shepherds enter.)

Song *(congregation):* "Away in a Manger"

Speaker: *(Reads Luke 2:8-20.)*

Song *(congregation):* "Silent Night! Holy Night!"

(Mary, Joseph, baby, angels and shepherds exit.)

Minister: Devotion on theme of "Keeping Christ in Christmas"

Poem: "The Priceless Gift of Christmas"
Song *(solo):* "Christmas in Your Heart"

Live Advent Wreath Program

Karen H. Whiting

This drama is easy to produce, using a few costumes and simple props. It explains the use of an advent wreath while focusing on the coming of Christ.

Costumes: Twelve to fifteen children wearing green with paper leaf collars or necklaces. Optional: a large green garland for children in green to hold. Five children in green will have speaking parts.

Five candle children in costumes:
Child 1: dressed as a prophet and carrying a Bible
Child 2: wears a star headpiece and holds a loaf of bread
Child 3: dressed as a shepherd and carrying a shepherd's staff or large candy cane
Child 4: wears an angel costume
Child 5 *(tallest child):* dressed in white and wearing a birthday hat or crown

Props: Five flashlights to represent candles to be held by the five candle children. Three lights covered in purple *(ribbon or paper)*; 1 in pink; and 1 in white.

(Open with all children in green standing in a line.)

Green Child 1: He's coming! Jesus is coming! The word advent means "coming." An advent wreath helps us prepare for the coming of Jesus at Christmas.

Green Child 2: The advent wreath combines the eternal circle, the evergreen of God's everlasting love, and the light of Jesus.

Green Child 3: We wear green. The green of growth as we grow close to God during advent.

Green Child 4: We wear the evergreen of the everlasting love of God.

Green Child 5: A circle has no beginning and no ending. God is eternal, and His love has no beginning or ending. When we give love, it circles back to us. The advent wreath is shaped in a circle.

(The children in green now form a circle, sitting down, legs crossed, to shape the wreath. The candle children enter one at a time, speak their part, then stand in place at the wreath, lighting their flashlight. The first four candle children will be evenly spaced around the wreath. The last one will stand in the center of the wreath.)

Candle Child 1: I am the candle of prophecy. As a prophet my words lit the way of the coming Messiah. I am only one lonely light. Prophets stood alone, proclaiming God's message. Christ's birth fulfilled all the prophecies about the Messiah's birth. Christmas is the celebration of the first coming of Christ and with it is the hope of His second coming.

This purple color is for repentance. As a prophet I called people to repent and prepare for the Messiah.

All sing: "O Come, O Come, Emmanuel"

Candle Child 2: I am the second candle of the advent wreath. I am called the Bethlehem candle. My glowing light reminds others of the light of the star the wise men followed. The star guided them to Bethlehem. Light is needed to guide us in darkness. We need the light of Christ to guide us every day. The glow of Christ's light should shine in our hearts always and reach out to others in need of His light.

My name, Bethlehem, means "house of bread." Jesus is the bread of life, our daily bread.

In Bethlehem, there was no room for Jesus except in a humble stable. Make sure there is room for Jesus in your heart and in your life.

All sing: "O Little Town of Bethlehem" or "Away in a Manger"

42

Candle Child 3: I am the third candle of the advent wreath, the Shepherd's candle. I am a different color, pink, to remind us of the great joy the shepherd's shared at the birth of Christ and our joy as we are so close to Christmas. Over half the candles are now lit, reminding us of the approaching nearness of Christmas!

   Shepherds were the first people to come worship Jesus. We shepherds responded with great joy as soon as we heard the news of Christ's birth. My light shines forth calling all to respond with joy!

   Jesus is the Good Shepherd and, as such, cares for us and guides us. The shepherd's staff guides the sheep. The candy cane is made of the red of love and white of purity entwined in the shape of the shepherd's staff.

All sing: "Silent Night" or "Joy to the World!" *(the first two verses)*

Candle Child 4: I am the fourth candle, the Angel candle. Angels are God's messengers. Angels announced the news of Christ's birth to others. We angels filled the sky with singing and rejoicing at Christ's birth. The wreath is now all aglow with light. People should have their hearts all aglow with the light of Christ.

   People are all called to be messengers, too. Take time to share the good news of Christ with others.

All sing: "Hark! the Herald Angels Sing"

Candle Child 5: I am the Christ candle. I am placed here on Christmas Day. I wear white because Jesus came into the world without sin, pure and holy.

   I am the tallest candle. The wise men looked in the sky and saw a brighter light than the other stars, recognizing that the heavens declared the birth of the King!

   Are you wise enough to look beyond the commercial sparkle at Christmas time to see the brighter light—the light of Christ that gives eternal life?

   I am in the center because Christ should be in the center of our lives.

All sing: "Happy Birthday" to Jesus!

Whitney Sees the Christ Child

Lillian Robbins

Characters

Narrator—an expressive reader
Mother
Dad
Whitney—boy or girl about 7 years old
Joseph
Mary
Innkeeper
First Traveler *(boy)*
Second Traveler *(boy)*
Woman Traveler
First Shepherd
Second Shepherd
Third Shepherd
Speaking Angel
Singing Angels *(as many as available)*

Scene I: Family's Living Room
Scene II: Bethlehem Inn
Scene III: Hillside of Bethlehem
Scene IV: Stable at Inn

Props: Recliner, chair and watch for Mom, small table, lamp, board game, gifts, Christmas bows, book, "NO VACANCY" sign, campfire, manger, straw, doll, stool for Mary, spotlight

Costumes: Angels' costumes, robes, bandanas or other appropriate headdress for Biblical scenes, staff for shepherds, makeup and clothes for Mother and Dad

Scene I

Christmas Eve. Whitney and Dad are sitting on the floor playing a game. Mother is wrapping gifts. This scene is at far side of stage.

Narrator *(as invisible as possible)*: It is Christmas Eve, and we join

Whitney's family in the living room of their home as they spend the last few hours before midnight.

Dad *(Whitney wiggles restlessly):* Whitney, can't you sit still so we can play this game?

Whitney: Yeah, but how much longer 'til Christmas?

Dad: It's just a few more hours, but you may as well settle down. Christmas won't be here until it gets here no matter how much you wiggle.

Mother: It's hard to believe that another Christmas is just a few hours away. And, Dad, just look how much our little boy has grown since last Christmas.

Dad: He sure has. Before I know it, he'll be wanting to play golf with me at the club.

Mother *(looks at her watch):* It's almost 9:00 o'clock. I think it's about time for you to go to bed, Whitney.

Whitney: I'm not sleepy, Mom.

Mother: You may think you're not sleepy, but it's time for bed.

Dad: Let's give him a few more minutes. We want to finish playing this game. If Whitney will just settle down, it won't take much longer.

Whitney *(after a few moments):* Yea, Dad, see that? I win. That makes three games for me.

Dad: I might have known. You're pretty good at this you know.

Mother: Okay, I think you better go to bed now, Whitney.

Whitney: But I just want to stay up a little longer! Please, Mom.

Dad *(yawning):* Well, I'm getting sleepy. It's bed for me. See you tomorrow. *(Dad takes the game and leaves the room.)*

Whitney: Mom, just let me finish reading this book I started before. *(Picks up book and opens it.)*

Mother: Well, I have a big day tomorrow. But if that's the way you want it, I'll just leave you sitting in that big chair. Are you going to be afraid to stay up by yourself?

Whitney: Of course not.

Mother: Good night then. See you on Christmas Day. *(Gives hug and leaves room. Whitney settles down in recliner.)*

Narrator: Whitney thinks he can stay awake, but he can't keep his eyes open. *(Whitney lays his head on the chair arm and closes his eyes.)* Now he has fallen asleep, and his head is full of dreams.

(Remove Mother's chair, table, and lamp.)

Scene II

Lights out in audience, dim on stage.

Narrator: Whitney's dream is so real, it is just like he is right there in the land of Israel. He dreams he can see a man walking across the fields, and he is leading a donkey. A woman sits on the donkey's back, and they are going over a hill somewhere between Nazareth and Bethlehem. Then a man's voice is heard.

Joseph *(strong voice from backstage):* Mary, I know you're getting tired, but it is just a little further now.

Mary *(from backstage):* I will be all right, Joseph, but I hope we get to the inn soon. I do want to get off this donkey.

Narrator: Mary and Joseph left Nazareth several days ago traveling to the City of David where Joseph must register for taxes because he is a descendant of David. This has been a long, tiresome trip for Mary. She has been riding on the donkey for many miles. Joseph doesn't mind walking beside the donkey, but he is concerned about Mary.

Many people pass Joseph and Mary along the road to Bethlehem, but Joseph must go slowly. Mary is jostled too much anyway. There is an inn located on the outskirts of Bethlehem. People are coming from all directions and flocking toward the door of the inn. *(Spotlight on inn.)*

(Traveler knocks on the door; innkeeper opens door.)

First Traveler: I want a room for the night.

Innkeeper: Do you have money?

First Traveler: Sure, no problem.

Innkeeper: Come on in then. *(They go inside.)*

Second Traveler *(accompanied by woman, knocks on door):* We have traveled all day long and need a room so we can sleep tonight.

Innkeeper: It'll cost you extra for the woman.

Second Traveler: I understand that, but my wife has to sleep some place, too. *(They go inside.)*

Joseph *(from backstage):* You wait Mary. I'll go and see about a room for the night.

(Joseph comes on stage and knocks at door.)

Narrator: It is getting dark as Joseph knocks at the door of the inn. There is no answer. He knocks again. No answer. Then Joseph knocks very loud, and the innkeeper comes to the door.

Joseph: I need a room for my wife and me.

Innkeeper: There is no room in this inn. *(Starts to close door.)*

Joseph: Wait a minute. You don't understand. My wife is very tired. We must have a place to rest.

Innkeeper: I told you; I don't have a vacant room!

Joseph: But we must do something. I can't just leave Mary sitting out there on the donkey. Please, help us!

Innkeeper: I am just the innkeeper! I can't work miracles!

Joseph: But it is time for Mary to deliver her firstborn child. We must have a place for shelter.

Innkeeper: If you want to go to the stables, you can find shelter there, and you can make a bed in the hay. *(The innkeeper goes inside, gets a "NO VACANCY" sign, hangs it outside, and goes back inside.)*

Joseph *(as he walks away):* I knew God would provide a place for His son to be born. *(Spotlight off inn.)*

Narrator: Whitney is suddenly awakened from his dream. *(Light on Whitney.)*

Whitney: Ooooooh! What was that? A dream I guess. Boy, I am sooooo sleepy! *(He balls up in Dad's chair again.)*

Scene III

Set up shepherds' campfire away from Whitney.

Narrator: Whitney is too sleepy to stay awake, but he will not go to bed. He hardly misses a wink before he starts to dream again. *(Shepherds on stage—spotlight on them.)* This time he dreams about shepherds in the field. There must be a hundred sheep on the side of the hill. The shepherds sit beside a campfire as they talk.

First Shepherd: What do you know, I didn't have a single sheep go astray today.

Third Shepherd: I thought I did, but it was just Pokey lagging way behind all the others.

First Shepherd: I was glad that stream had not dried up. It seems to me we had a pretty good day, don't you think so?

Second Shepherd: Looks like this is going to be a good night, too. I think I'm just going to settle in early, though. *(Stands up and starts to leave the campfire.)*

Third Shepherd: Yeah, I like these cool nights.

First Shepherd *(looking up):* You know the sky looks strange. Many a night I've sat under these stars, but somehow it is different tonight. *(All look up at sky.)*

Narrator: Suddenly a strange light shines in the sky. *(Bright spotlight.)* A white figure appears before the shepherds. *(Angel appears.)*

Angel: Men, don't be afraid. I just came to tell you about a baby boy just born in Bethlehem in a stable. He is wrapped in swaddling clothes and lying in a manger. This special baby is Christ, the Lord, the Savior of the world.

Narrator: Suddenly, the whole sky is filled with angels. *(Angels appear from as many directions as possible.)* They are singing the most beautiful song the shepherds ever heard.

(Angels, with tape, sing "Gloria." When singing stops, angels leave.)

Second Shepherd: The angel said the Christ child was born in Bethlehem. Let's go and see this Savior of the world.
(They leave stage. Spotlight off.)

Scene IV

(Remove campfire. Set up nativity scene.)
Whitney *(rubbing his eyes):* Boy! That was some dream. I wonder if I could get back into it. *(Settles down again.)*
Narrator: Whitney is fascinated with his dream, and immediately closes his eyes hoping to keep that dream going. This time he doesn't see the hills where the sheep graze. *(A dim light appears on the manger scene.)* He looks at the stable. He thinks he hears a baby cry, but it is dark. He can't see very well. Whitney is restless in his sleep. *(Whitney squirms.)* He wants so much to see what is in that stable.

Then the crying stops, *(Spotlight on manger.)* and Whitney can see the baby. He thinks there is a smile on his face. Joseph is standing nearby, and there is Mary sitting beside the manger. Then he knows. This is the baby that the angels have been talking about.

Whitney wonders what has happened to the shepherds. He peers into the darkness, and far away, he can see men walking across the field. The shepherds; they are coming to see baby Jesus. *(Shepherds appear and approach the manger.)* They kneel at the manger and bow their heads as they worship Jesus, the Son of God. *(Light on manger fades away.)*
Whitney *(almost falls out of the chair, then jumps up):* I wish I could have been there! *(Calls toward the door.)* Mom! Dad! Come quick!
Mother *(as she and Dad rush in):* What is it, Whitney? What happened?
Whitney: Something really super! I saw baby Jesus lying in the manger. And I saw Mary and Joseph. The angels were singing, and the shepherds came to the stable. It was all so exciting!
Dad: You know, Whitney, that is the reason we celebrate Christmas— because Jesus was born. We celebrate Christmas to remember that God sent Jesus because He loves everybody in the whole world. Jesus is God's gift, the best one anybody can ever receive.
Whitney: Mom, I'm ready to go to bed now. I don't really want to stay up any longer. *(They exit the stage. "Silent Night" is heard from backstage as the spotlight is on the nativity scene.)*